Article Marketing Skills

Benard Ogola

ISBN: 9798355340506

DEDICATION

I dedicate this work to my dad Sylvester Oboth who often criticized me but paid for my tuition until I graduated from university.

I dedicate this work to my daughter Benedict Agola and my nephew Kevin Ochola for have always loved what I do. Thank you for your encouraging words.

CONTENTS

ACKNOWLEDGMENTS

I like to express my special thanks and gratitude to my father, Sylvester Oboth, my mother, Judith Oboth, and siblings, Anthony Japian, Susan Agola, Pamela Amollo, and Benjamin Obango. I will not forget the great support they gave me and for encouraging me to focus on what I am writing to be successful in my writing career.

I also send special thanks to my daughter Benedict Agola and my nephew Kevin Ochola for provoking me by stealing my laptop to type their own stories and articles whenever I was doing other research and assignments elsewhere. I would always find funny writings on my page that were annoying, kept me laughing, and encouraged me to write better.

As always, thank you for the financial support you extended to me when my laptop got damaged during my trip to Queen Elizabeth national park, located in katurungu, Kasese district, in western Uganda.

Thank you!

DISCLAIMER:

This ebook has been researched and compiled with the intent to provide information for persons wishing to learn about making a profit using various online resources.

The Publisher has endeavored to be as accurate as possible in the creation of this report, notwithstanding the fact that he does not warrant or represent at any time that the contents within are accurate due to the changing nature of the internet.

While all attempts have been made to verify information provided in this book, the Publisher assumes no responsibility for errors, omissions, or contrary interpretation of the subject matter herein.

All content, products, and services are not to be considered as legal, financial, or professional advice and are to be used for personal use and information purposes only. The purpose is to educate and guide.

Readers are cautioned to reply on their own judgment about their individual circumstances to act accordingly as the publishers expressly disclaim any liability arising from any strategies, techniques, and advice presented in this ebook.

CHAPTER 1

INTRODUCTION

Before we start, let me tell you the meaning of traffic. The word traffic in marketing is "customer", coming to your website or product page and creating the possibility of more likeliness to buy your product. They are your readers or audience.

Organic traffic is not, having to pay for adverts run on online sites and other social media sites like Facebook, YouTube, Twitter, LinkedIn, and the more recent ones, Instagram, Tiktok and Snapchat.

There are many things you should put in your mind while writing an article with the aim of marketing and exposure in various article directories and making good profits out of your efforts.

What you should know is that writing just about anything may not get you expected results not until you perform keyword research to identify what the target audience and readers are looking for online for you to have a good marketing campaign.

To get good traffic from your articles, you need to incorporate the keywords your target audience is searching for online into your content and submit them to the article directories.

You will position yourself very well in search engines, and your readers will be your target customers.

CHAPTER 2

CHOOSING YOUR TARGET MARKET

There are many ways you can go about researching and evaluating keywords and phrases to use in your articles, the shortest time possible would be 15 to 20 minutes of concentration.

Keep in your mind;

1. The market you plan to target
2. And the products you decide to promote.

Come up with a list of hot topics with several existing products to promote as an affiliate or create products yourself by browsing the marketplace for products to promote.

You can browse clickbank marketplace for high converting digital products that you can start to promote immediately.

To be a successful article marketer promoting affiliate-based digital products would be a good start.

We are using clickbank basically because it's the largest marketplace for digital products. If you find the payment system is unfavorable or won't allow money transfer/wire to your country, you can use other marketplaces available.

Just register with them and start your affiliate article marketing. Below are other affiliate marketplaces.

MARKET PLACES:

- ClickBank
  It's an affiliate network and a
  marketplace where you can find
  thousands of digital products to
  promote.

- Amazon Associates
  Amazon is a big retailer in the world. All
  you need to do is to have a website or
  social media account and sign up for
  their affiliate marketing program known
  as Amazon Associates so that you
  monetize your websites and social media
  pages.

- eBay
  It's the world's largest action
  marketplace where you can get well-
  priced products.

- ShareASale
  Purely an affiliate marketing network
  that offers pay-per-lead affiliates
  marketing.

- Commission Junction A leader in the affiliate marketing industry allows affiliates to engage shoppers through their websites, blogs, social media, and other technologies.

- Rakuten Affiliate
Very famous for offering cash back, deals, and shopping rewards on a selection of products and services offered at their stores.

- Shopify.com
Shopify is a place for independent business owners looking to make good profits.

- Bluehost.com
Blue host is one of the leading web hosting companies in the world. It provides various tools and fair web hosting packages.

- Leadpages
Landpages provide businesses with easy leads and make sales. They offer websites, landing pages, pop-ups, and many more.

- WarriorPlus
With WarriorPlus you can create, sell and market your digit products.

After evaluating and researching any market, carefully focus on these four elements.

1. Whether there are desperate buyers in the market who are willing and eager to buy a solution to an existing problem.

2. The size of the market whether there are buyers purchasing products and services within the niche.

3. Whether the current competition within the market is not too thick to penetrate.

4. The quantity and quality of the products in the market should be in abundance to promote in your campaigns.

Once you are inside the clickbank marketplace, enter the keywords and phrases of the products you want to promote, alternatively browse through the recently added products marketplace or the already existing categories.

The marketplace listing features products with specific information regarding current stats.

Understand it in this way;

$/sale: The amount of money you earn for each sale.

 Future $: Average rebills revenue.
Total $/sale: Average total $ per sale, including all, rebills.

 %/sale: The percentage of the product sale price that the sale represents.

 %/refd: Fraction of publisher's total sales that are referred by affiliates.

Grav: The measure of how many affiliates are promoting the product.

You will know how better a product is selling through the gravity indicator as a gravity indicator of 100 will mean the product is doing better than that of gravity 20.

So it's better to focus on what is selling now to make it easy for you to come up with product ideas and to know the topics to write about.

When within the marketplace, the system will generate a link (Hoplink) that is customized and designed for every affiliate and a specific product, which you can only generate if you have signed, up for an account.

Browse through the different categories in the genres and market niche, write down each topic of your interest that is on-demand, create your Hoplink, copy and paste it into your text file so that you can use it in your landing pages.

This is what they mean by Hoplinks:

Product
 Hoplink:
http://your_id.product.hop.clickbank.net/

Mobile Phone
Hoplink:
http://xxxx.mphone.hop.clickbank.net/

To be successful you have to dominate the various article directories with articles of the products that you promote so that you can beat your competitors.

Let's have a review of what we have learned about article marketing to drive organic traffic to your website or any other affiliate product marketplace that you promote.

1. First, find a product to promote by doing a keyword search of the product of your interest.

2. Do multi-keyword searches to find out what products, topics, and phrases people search for on the internet.

    Find out if the product is currently hot by visiting the marketplace to see the list rankings and if you find a product that you like but has a bad ranking, don't attempt to even try it.

    It's always advisable to find a product of your interest to promote before you even think about a keyword search and by making sure the product is hot.

You are always good to go if the sale page is working well, has a good commission and the product owner is easily contactable.

Good affiliate's commissions in the marketplaces often range from 50% to 70% that is if the owner is much interested in the product to moving very fast.

CHAPTER 3

HOW MANY ARTICLES YOU SHOULD WRITE

You ought to make it a hobby to write several articles every day for every product you find to promote and saturate them in the various directories.

When you have decided the product and market niche you are going into, consider doing keyword and phrase research so that you can create articles that are of good quality.

If you are promoting specific products consider integrating the product title and the authors' name into some of your articles so that you can generate targeted leads from those searching for information on these products.

It's a good blend if your articles end up in review platforms where you offer detailed information regarding specific products; you will be on a good track as there are already desperate buyers waiting to buy the products but were only waiting for more information.

Researching and evaluating keywords, you will need to begin with; <u>Google Keyword Planner.</u>

Enter the keyword phrases that describe the market, topics, and products of your choice that you are planning to promote including the product titles and authors' names.

The Google keyword planner allows you to enter all phrases and keywords from your chosen market niche and evaluate your competition based on online search.

Google keyword planner allows you to generate listings that bring out various keywords associated with the one you are searching for or have entered into the search box.

Ironically, the first column provides you with different keywords that you can use within your content, search engine, and as well promoting products within the pay clicks (PPC) marketplace.

The second column indicates the level of competition.
And the third column indicates the monthly estimated number of searches for every keyword.

Keyword search takes time but as one becomes used and with experience, everything is quick and simple each time one is developing a content campaign.

It allows you to generate keyword listings from those used by your competitors within the campaigns and the marketplaces and which ones are ranking.

You will also be able to evaluate specific keyword phrases based on the number of websites that feature these keywords content in their websites.

Other keyword tools and resources available
  http://trends.google.com/

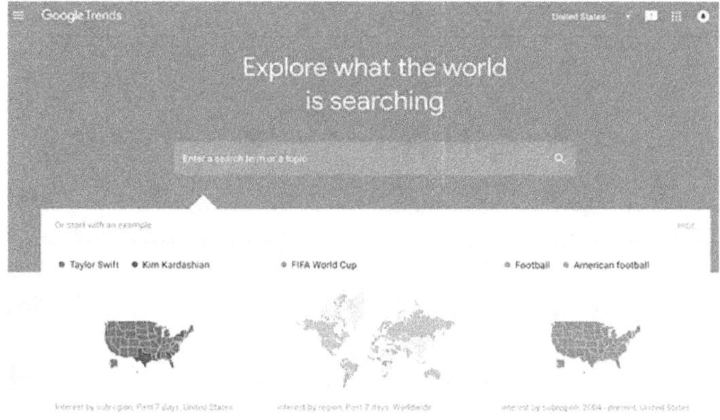

The website will be displayed according to the popularity of specific search phrases and keyword terms.

If you enter in a keyword search it will show you exactly how many people are searching for that keyword.

It's a nice tool to determine how popular a niche market is, and how which keywords are commonly searched.

WORDTRACKER
This one tool is the most known and popular keyword tool. It gives you a variety of keywords but is not accurate in terms of traffic.

In order to get an accurate reflection of the total number of searches on Google, and all major search engines, you should endeavor to multiply the numbers it gives you by around 3-10.

The paid version will get you unlimited keywords at a time; however, a free version is available at wordtracker that will generate 100 keywords at a time.

YAHOO ANSWERS
To evaluate the level of competition for various keywords, you can also use the major search engines by directly entering in your keyword phrase, like this; Yahoo

It's a very intelligent way to locate a variety of questions that people are looking for answers to.

You can register a free Yahoo Answers account and answer open questions, (including your website link within the resource box), and also browse trends to usual niche topics that people are interested in.

Once you are ready with the niche topics that you plan to write about, you will need to ensure that your articles are crafted to rank well in the search engines.

Your target phrases in Google search engines in "quotes" should have less than 150,000 search results when you search for them in keyword phrases. Let's say "how to stop smoking".

Organic article marketing is not hard especially when you use the tools available to reduce the time required to write and saturate your articles to the various directories.

CHAPTER 4

YOUR ARTICLE MAKING PROFITS

Begin with opening an Ezine Articles Account, if you don't have one, however, if you have one you will need to make some changes to get the best performance possible out of your account.

Ezine articles manually approve each article you submit to their site and if your 10 articles have been approved, then you will be able to enjoy submitting an unlimited number of articles.

You will have to fill out a form at your first registration including your email address, password, first and last name, and address.

Be sure to fill in the correct detail as they can reject your registration if you provide them with invalid information.

Fill out your authors' profile and add a photo of yourself, add a couple of links to your resource box, focusing Only On One Website Per Article to avoid making it difficult for readers to know which website to visit, when they need particular information regarding your current article. The resource box is the most important part as it has links directing your audience to your site.

There is a video tutorial guide on the site in case you have registration problems but once account setup is successful, enter your email address and login password to access your account details.

Email Address

Password   Forgot Password?

Sign In

You will be able to submit articles from your administration panel and once you have a handful of approved articles, you can check for current stats including article views, ratings, and what articles are ranking higher than others just from the drop-down menu under "Author Tools

Focus on creating high converting articles for better statistics that generate traffic to your websites using the many features available to you from within the administrative panel.

The site allows you to add additional authors to your account, if you wish to write under different pen names, catering to multiple markets.

When you log into your account, you will see an account overview on the left-hand side with stats that will resemble this:

This box shows how many of your articles were approved, and are "live" (visible), how many times your articles were viewed, the times your profile was viewed, and the clicks generated as a result of your articles.

CHAPTER 5

THE URL CLICKS

This is the link (https://www.com) that you provided in your articles. It's very useful because it's what directs readers to the landing pages or websites and the higher the number of clicks the better your articles are performing on the internet.

Our primary aim is to encourage people to click on the URL and that is why you should spend enough time evaluating your articles to know which categories are performing better.

Go through others articles and take time to find out what other people are searching for using selector tools available to you.

You should write original articles by only referencing others' articles and avoid plagiarizing others' articles for you to be a successful writer and beat your competition.

It's as easy as reading someone's article and writing your original article by filling n the gaps that were left out.

You don't have to be the best writer but you have to get ahead of your competition by dominating your article all over the directories.

Practice makes perfect, and therefore to increase speed write many articles a day, at worst 4 to 5 articles an hour. You should be able to create a 300-word article in 15 minutes.

CHAPTER 6

DEVELOPING THE IDEA

Click the URL http://www.ezinearticles.com, search for articles on topics you want to write about, pass through them quickly and write your own original articles and circulate them to get more traffic.

ARTICLE QUALITY VS ARTICLE QUANTITY

Just write many articles for your readers to read and click on the links you provided for you to make more money. Use simple words that won't confuse your audience but encourage them to read the whole article. The system is simple, readers need information.

If you can't write, you can outsource writers by heading to freelance marketplaces to get seasoned writers to help you with good articles of your market niche.

In fact, if you outsource writers, you will have enough time to work on your website or your landing pages so that when visitors arrive after reading your articles, you can convert them to customers and even subscribers.

FREELANCE MARKERTPLACES:

http://www.Guru.com
http://www.GetAFreelancer.com
https://www.upwork.com
http://www.Constant-Content.com

You should have a habit of writing articles each day and submitting them in the leading directory http://www.ezinearticles.com which will bring your enough traffic.

One good point to remember is your articles should always have the same writing style. If you outsourced them, always use the same writer because people always prefer the specific writing style.

Head on http://forums.digitalpoint.com, a free marketplace to post content for sale, to locate prewritten articles on any market niche.

CHAPTER 7

ROLLING THE CONTENT

After you have chosen what to write about, the products, and put together the keywords, then you are more than ready to write and submit you're to article directories.

Choosing the market and products could have been somehow a task but by now you need to write or outsource some articles on specific topics you are going to write about.

Ensure your articles connect directly to the topics you write about. Don't write an article about "Dog walking" and place a link to a product selling "weight loss". The product and the topic of your article need to be connected too close.

Keep the length of your article to about 300 to 400 words to entice people to read them and click on the link at the author's resource box directing them to a landing page or website with your affiliate link.

What you should know is that writing just about anything may not get you expected results not until you perform keyword research to identify what the target audience and readers are looking for online for you to have a good marketing campaign.

To get good traffic from your articles, you need to incorporate the keywords your target audience is searching for online into your content and submit them to the article directories.

You will position yourself very well in search engines, and your readers will be your target customers.

Everything begins with researching and evaluating whether a market niche is profitable or not before you start spending your time creating your marketing articles and driving traffic to your desired links.

CHAPTER 8

THE ARTICLE

Three parts make up a good article;

<u>The Title</u>
The first thing your readers will always see is your article title. You must concentrate much on your article title as it serves as the headline to your sales page. Make it irresistible and attention-grabbing.

<u>Article Description</u>
When article directories submit your content to their database, the titles and descriptions are the first parts of your paragraph within your article that will come up.

<u>Body content</u>
The article body should drive your readers till the end by you making it interesting, on-topic keeping the length to about 400 words, and making a summarized conclusion at the end of the last paragraph.

Your article should;

- Be very clear with a title that grabs the reader's attention instantly.

- Write the paragraph while clearly describing the topics of your article.

- Keep the body interesting so that people read all through the end of your story.

- Have good closing remarks prompting your readers to read the resource box.

At the resource box, people should be able to click on the links provided to lead them by offering a free report or eBook or something relevant to the topic of your article.

Sometimes you are not sure whether your article is giving away too much content to the readers or not, which is why you should use a simple system to solve that problem.

1.   Introduction
Clearly explain to your readers what the article is about, adding all the benefits and aids if available.

2.   Subject matter
Provide examples to your topic putting in both positive and negative aspects.

3.   And the solution to the subject matter. Lastly, provide the possible solution and how to get started.

CHAPTER 9

WRITING A COMPELLING RESOURCE BOX

You need to spend enough time evaluating how best you will use the small space at the resource box that will motivate your readers to click on your link and visit your website.

As an author the resource box is the only limited space that allows you to promote your product, so you must invoke a call of action and entice readers to follow through and click the resource box.

With EzineArticles, you can create multiple author accounts and create multiple resource boxes that accomplish and cover each article that you write.

Offer your readers an incentive to click through your resource box by giving them a free giveaway like;

- A free report
- Free eBook
- Newsletter or subscription
- Free Trial of membership

■   And the free sample of a paid product. Use anchor text to rank within the search engines for specific keywords and phrases about your market niche.

Incorporate a call of action directing your readers to click through and explore your squeeze, landing pages, or website.

Here is an example of a compelling resource box:

I specialize in teaching people how to make the most money out of their article writing.

To gain access to tools where you can learn how to make more money from your article marketing, click the link below https://www.your-website.com - (leading to your landing pages or website with a free giveaway).

To have an anchor text, use the cursor to select the word, right-click, go to hypertext and add the URL you want to use i.e. https://www.your-website.com. Or/ Landing pages.

CHAPTER 10

QUICK ACTION PLAN

If you follow this plan, you are on your way to earning $200 to $300 a day with article marketing and affiliate-based products.

Clickbank is the biggest marketplace for selling digital products but you can as well choose from the various marketplaces already told to you in this article.

New products are being added daily and you can spend your time evaluating polarity, gravity and the performance of each product by using the free clickbank resources http://www.CBEngine.com and http://www.CBTrends.com available to your disposal.

To make sure you are being compensated for your efforts, don't promote products that pay you less than 50% commission.

To find a list of affiliate programs that pay often, here is a quick resource to use http://www.lifetimecommissions.com

1. The keyword list
    Compile your keyword list with not less than 25 keywords per topic so that you have a swipe file available whenever you want to write more articles.

2. Write the article.
    After you have chosen the product, compiled your keyword list, create and submit your articles. The more high-quality articles in circulation, the more exposure you will receive.

    Just make sure the product is relevant to the market and that you are focused on your articles and speaking directly to the customer.

    Write 10 to 20 articles on each topic or product you plan to promote and circulate to the directories. You can use a tool like an article marketing robot.

3. Create landing pages and submit your articles.
    Create high-converting landing pages and squeeze pages and give away free eBooks to

your readers for them to subscribe to your mailing list.

Place these links to the author's resource box with a call of action enticing your readers to explore your product page or website. Focus on building a mailing list after capturing their information and contact them later.

Many people hate giving away their email and to do so give out something for free and they will eventually give their email in exchange.

Also after they have given their email, make a follow-up email to them using a professional autoresponder like www.Aweber.com or www.GetResponse.com

There are other autoresponders out there that you can use. Once you have created your articles, submit them to https://www.ezinearticles.com/ and other article directories as well.

4. Double-check your keywords.
        After you have submitted a number of your articles double-check the keywords to see which articles are performing best and which ones you need to weed out.

This can often be done by going back to the article directories, checking, and evaluating the stats.

Create your article marketing system so that you read out to new readers by having several articles in circulation which will potentially lead to more sales.

As a new marketer, your article marketing is for brand development and awareness by generating targeted traffic for you. Ensure consistency by adding fresh new articles to the directories each week for you to get more exposure.

Make sure your articles are easy to read, have the correct spelling, are well paragraphed, and that you are communicating directly to the readers who are searching products out there.

With a squeeze and landing pages, you will be able to build your targeted list of subscribers, send out broadcasts and emails containing affiliate-based product links.

Article marketing is an effective way of getting lots of traffic to your website, building a list, branding, and developing your network and reputation.

Just take action and you will be ahead of your competition.

TOOLS AND RESOURCES

http://www.EzineArticles.com

http://www.ArticleDashboard.com

http://www.ArticlesBase.com

http://www.ArticleCube.com

http://www.IdeaMarketers.com

http://www.ArticleAlley.com

http://www.ArticleBiz.com

http://www.ArticlesFactory.com

http://www.Amazines.com

http://www.Buzzle.com

PUBLIC DOMAIN (FREE CONTENT)

https://www.gutenberg.org/

https://www.ipl.org/

http://www.searchebooks.com/

Success in your Article Marketing!

ABOUT THE AUTHOR

I'm a copywriter and marketer but carry professionalism in Journalism, accounting, and web programming. I spend most of my time online researching, helping businesses with marketing, and realizing their social media presence.

As an entrepreneur consultant, I create products and services around my expertise that solve problems and bring results to various businesses I work alongside. SaaS is a Gig!

I love what I do, particularly when I take my time researching various writing and marketing topics. That means I am always crafting new business content for my audience and sending emails to people that compel them to take action.

Throughout my career, I have had the privilege to write copy for businesses across distinct industries, not limited to hotels, travel, healthcare, and technology.